SKIRRID HILL

By the same author

Poetry
The Blue Book

Non-fiction
The Dust Diaries

Drama
Unicorns, almost

Skirrid Hill
Owen Sheers

seren
in association with
THE WORDSWORTH TRUST

Seren is the book imprint of Poetry Wales Press Ltd
Nolton Street, Bridgend, Wales
www.seren-books.com

Typeset in Monotype Dante by
Craig Birtles for the Wordsworth Trust
www.wordsworth.org.uk

© Copyright Owen Sheers, 2005
First published in 2005
Reprinted in February 2006

The right of Owen Sheers to be identified as the Author
of this work has been asserted in accordance
with the Copyright, Designs
and Patents Act, 1988

ISBN 1-85411-403-4

A CIP record for this title is available from the British Library

Printed by CPD, Ebbw Vale

A note on the title

Skirrid: from the Welsh *Ysgyrid*, a derivation of *Ysgariad* meaning divorce or separation.

Acknowledgements

Acknowledgements are due to the editors of the following publications in which some of these poems first appeared: *www.boomeranguk.com*, *Oxford Poetry*, *www.poems.com*, *Poetry Review*, *Poetry Wales*, *Rattlepax*, *South West Review*, *The Times*, *Zembla*.

'Stitch in Time' was commissioned for BBC Radio 3's 'The Verb' and was first published in *Out of Fashion* edited by Carol Ann Duffy (Faber, 2004). 'Hedge School' and 'Service' were both commissioned by The Poetry Society for National Poetry Day 2004. 'History' and 'Liable to Floods' were written as part of the Dolwyddelan Project, organised and funded by Bob Borzello. 'The Fishmonger' arose from the British Council's 2004 British-Hungarian 'Converging Lines' project and 'Marking Time' was first performed in Bratislava, Slovakia as part of the Ars Poetica poetry festival. 'Flag' was previously published in *Twentieth Century Anglo-Welsh Poetry* edited by Dannie Abse (Seren, 2004). 'Swallows' was first published in *Wading Through Deep Water* edited by Tony Curtis (Coychurch Press, 2002) and an early version of 'Winter Swans' appears in *A Winter Garland* (The Wordsworth Trust, 2003).

Additional thanks are due to the Arts Council of England for a Grant for the Arts and for a Writer's Award.

For their criticism and advice on this manuscript I am especially grateful to Sarah Hall, Paul Henry, Matthew Hollis and Zoe Waldie. I'd also like to thank Charles and Camilla Smith for their generosity and understanding, Dr Robert Woof and the staff at The Wordsworth Trust for my time in the Lakes, and all the *First Liners* for good times on the road.

Last Act

Don't be surprised it has taken so long
to show you these:
the gaps like missing teeth
in the face of my speech,
the silent mouthing O,
the stuck record of my tongue
and the countdown through the page
to the zero of the word
failing to catch. Because
isn't this always the last act?
The drawing back of the curtain
to show the parts we've played.
The previous scenes stacked in the wings
and at the centre, under the spotlight,
the actor, bowing as himself
for the first time all night.

for Siân

'As we grow older
The world becomes stranger, the pattern more complicated
Of dead and living.'

T.S. Eliot, *East Coker*

Contents

Mametz Wood

For years afterwards the farmers found them –
the wasted young, turning up under their plough blades
as they tended the land back into itself.

A chit of bone, the china plate of a shoulder blade,
the relic of a finger, the blown
and broken bird's egg of a skull,

all mimicked now in flint, breaking blue in white
across this field where they were told to walk, not run,
towards the wood and its nesting machine guns.

And even now the earth stands sentinel,
reaching back into itself for reminders of what happened
like a wound working a foreign body to the surface of the skin.

This morning, twenty men buried in one long grave,
a broken mosaic of bone linked arm in arm,
their skeletons paused mid dance-macabre

in boots that outlasted them,
their socketed heads tilted back at an angle
and their jaws, those that have them, dropped open.

As if the notes they had sung
have only now, with this unearthing,
slipped from their absent tongues.

The Farrier

Blessing himself with his apron,
the leather black and tan of a rain-beaten bay,
he pinches a roll-up to his lips and waits

for the mare to be led from the field to the yard,
the smoke slow-turning from his mouth
and the wind twisting his sideburns in its fingers.

She smells him as he passes, woodbine, metal and hoof,
careful not to look her in the eye as he runs his hand
the length of her neck, checking for dust on a lintel.

Folding her back leg with one arm, he leans into her flank
like a man putting his shoulder to a knackered car,
catches the hoof between his knees

as if it's always just fallen from a table,
cups her fetlock and bends,
a romantic lead dropping to the lips of his lover.

Then the close work begins; cutting moon-sliver clippings,
excavating the arrow head of her frog,
filing at her sole and branding on a shoe

in an apparition of smoke,
three nails gritted between his teeth,
a seamstress pinning the dress of the bride.

Placing his tools in their beds,
he gives her a slap and watches her leave,
awkward in her new shoes, walking on strange ground.

The sound of his steel, biting at her heels.

Inheritance

After R.S. Thomas

From my father a stammer
like a stick in the spokes of my speech.
A tired blink,
a need to have my bones
near the hill's bare stone.
An affection for the order of maps
and the chaos of bad weather.

From my mother
a sensitivity to the pain in the pleasure.
The eye's blue ore,
quiet moments beside a wet horse
drying in a rain-loud stable.
A joiner's lathe
turning fact into fable.

And from them both –
a desire for what they forged
in their shared lives;
testing it under the years' hard hammer,
red hot at its core,
cooled dark at its sides.

Marking Time

That mark upon your back is finally fading
in the way our memory will,
of that night our lust wouldn't wait for bed
so laid us out upon the floor instead
where we worked up that scar –
two tattered flags flying from your spine's mast,
a brand-burn secret in the small of your back.

I trace them now and feel the disturbance again.
The still waters of your skin broken, the *volte* engaging
as we made our marks like lovers who carve trees,
the equation of their names equalled by an arrow
that buckles under time but never leaves,
and so though changed, under the bark, the skin,
the loving scar remains.

Show

I

The models walk,
high-heeled as curlews
stalking a narrow shore.

We watch, spectators
at a slow-motion tennis match,
as they turn,

flex the featherless wings
of their shoulders
and slip between the curtains,

leaving the crocodile pit of cameras
flashing their teeth for more.

II

I leave you sitting to the mirror
like a pianist to the piano,
lifting the mascara brush
to paint your lashes from fine to bold.

Pulling the door on this scene
I walk down the corridor
to wait in the bar for you to join me.
And when you do, it happens once more;

The fall of the dress, the jewellery,
early stars against the dusk of your skin,
all of it leaves me surrendered,
if just for a second, as you walk in,

to the spell, the artful hocus-pocus,
and to you standing there
one shoulder bare,
setting the room about you out of focus.

Valentine

The water torture of your heels
emptying before me down that Paris street,
evacuated as the channels of our hearts.

That will be one memory.

The swing of the tassels on your skirt
each step filling out the curve of your hip;
your wet lashes, the loss of everything we'd learnt.

That will be another.

Then later – holding each other on the hotel bed
like a pair of wrecked voyagers
who had thought themselves done for,

only to wake washed up on the shore
uncertain in their exhaustion
whether to laugh or weep.

That my valentine, will be the one I'll keep.

Winter Swans

The clouds had given their all –
two days of rain and then a break
in which we walked,

the waterlogged earth
gulping for breath at our feet
as we skirted the lake, silent and apart,

until the swans came and stopped us
with a show of tipping in unison.
As if rolling weights down their bodies to their heads

they halved themselves in the dark water,
icebergs of white feather, paused before returning again
like boats righting in rough weather.

'They mate for life' you said as they left,
porcelain over the stilling water. I didn't reply
but as we moved on through the afternoon light,

slow-stepping in the lake's shingle and sand,
I noticed our hands, that had, somehow,
swum the distance between us

and folded, one over the other,
like a pair of wings settling after flight.

Night Windows

That night we turned some of them off
but left the hall bulb bright,
sending one bar of light into the living room,
so we could see.

Which of course meant they could too –
us impressionist through the thin white drapes
as you lowered yourself to me,
the curves of a distant landscape

opening across your pelvis,
your body slick and valleyed
in the August heat
and your back arching like a bow

drawn by an invisible tendon
strung from the top of your head
to the ends of your toes,
loading you with our meeting.

The night windows opposite performed
their Morse codes,
side-swipes of curtains,
until eventually every one of them went dark

and the only light left was a siren's,
sending its blue strobe across the rooftops
like lightning in the corner of my eye,
somewhere far away yet near,

as with a sigh you rose from me
and walked into the lit hallway,
trailing the dress of your shadow behind you.

Keyways

Strange then, that this should be our last time together.
Standing in line at the locksmith's
waiting for a set of your keys to be cut
so I can visit your flat when you're out
and take back all that's mine again.

The hot day outside presses to the shop window glass,
lights the uncut sets along the wall
like lucky charms along a bracelet.
And I realise that's how I felt when we first met –
an uncut key, a smooth blade, edentate,

waiting your impression, the milling and grooves
of moments in time, until our keyways would fit,
as they finally did in that chapel, our breaths
rising and falling in unison as we listened to the *Messiah*,
touching at elbow, shoulder and hip

like a pair of Siamese twins sharing one lung.
From then on I was sure we were keyed alike.
That our combinations matched,
our tumblers aligned precisely to give and roll perfectly
into the other's empty spaces.

And at night, when you slept facing away from me
and I held the bow of your hip,
again it was a coming home, my stomach, the small of your back,
my knees in the hollows of yours, a master key fit.
So when did the bolt slip? The blade break in the mouth?

Useless now, I understand, to try and unpick the months
back to that second when, for the first time,
one of us made a turn that failed to dock,
went nowhere, stuck half-way, leaving us
waiting the expected click, which never came.

So strange then, that we should do this now,
this cutting of keys, just when we're changing all the locks.

Border Country

Nothing marks the car quarry now,
just raised earth like the hummock of a grave,
a headstone of trees, wind-written epitaphs
running in their leaves.
Filled in years ago,
but still I can't help standing at its edge,
where the ground once gave
to an elephant's graveyard of cars,
a motorway pile-up in the corner of the field.

One of the places we came
when we had tired of catching
the commas and apostrophes
of minnows and bullheads;
or shooting at pumpkins in the field,
shouldering the kick of your father's shotgun;
or playing at war in the barn,
dying again and again
under its gap-toothed roof and broken beams.

A place where we tested our voices,
young as the buzzards above us
striking their cries against a flint sky,
smashed black holes in the windows,
sat in the drivers' seats, going nowhere,
operated on engines,
dock-leaves and nettles running in their pistons
or just walked among them,
reading aloud from the names of the dead:

Volvo, Ford, Vauxhall,
their primary colours rusting to red.
Where we lost ourselves in the hours before dark,
year on year, until that day
when life put on the brakes
and pitched you, without notice,
through the windscreen of your youth.
Your father found at dawn –
a poppy sown in the unripe corn.

I came back once, to find the cars smaller
or the undergrowth grown,
whichever, the whole diminished to steel and stone.
Just cars in a quarry,
their dashboards undone and the needles
of the speedos settled at zero.
As I climbed back out I disturbed a buzzard
that flew from its branch like a rag
shaken out in the wind,

before spiralling upwards
above the shuffling trees
and on over the fields –
the spittle sheep, the ink-dot cows,
a tractor writing with its wheels,
and on over the lanes, where a boy
meandered between the hedges,
trailing a stick, kicking a stone,
trying once more to find his way home.

Farther

I don't know if the day after Boxing Day has a name
but it was then we climbed the Skirrid again,
choosing the long way round,
through the wood, simplified by snow,
along the dry stone wall, its puzzle solved by moss,
and out of the trees into that cleft of earth
split they say by a father's grief
at the loss of his son to man.
We stopped there at an altar of rock and rested,
watching the dog shrink over the hill before continuing ourselves,
finding the slope steeper than expected.
A blade of wind from the east
and the broken stone giving under our feet
with the sound of a crowd sighing.
Half way up and I turned to look at you,
your bent head the colour of the rocks,
your breath reaching me, short and sharp and solitary,
and again I felt the tipping in the scales of us,
the intersection of our ages.
The dog returns having caught nothing but his own tongue
and you are with me again, so together we climbed to the top
and shared the shock of a country unrolled before us,
the hedged fields breaking on the edge of Wales.
Pulling a camera from my pocket I placed it on the trig point
and leant my cheek against the stone to find you in its frame,
before joining you and waiting for the shutter's blink
that would tell me I had caught this:
the sky rubbed raw over the mountains,
us standing on the edge of the world, together against the view
and me reaching for some kind of purchase
or at least a shallow handhold in the thought
that with every step apart, I'm another closer to you.

Trees

You tell me you've planted an oak
in the middle of the top field.

When I ask how long before
it'll be fully grown, you nod your head

and say 'some time'
and I realise I should have known.

After all, you planted trees for our arrivals,
one for each of us at the north, south and west of the house,

and now you have planted this –
a finger-thick sapling drawn by the breeze into a long bow

loaded with the promise of what it will become,
silhouetted against a reddening sky

that could be the setting or the rising of a sun.

Hedge School

'Though that hir soules goon a-blakeberyed'
                              Chaucer, *The Pardoner's Prologue*

The walk home from school got longer
those first weeks of September,
listening to the mini bus diminish
through the hedges and trees,
then slipping the straps of my bag over each shoulder
to free up both hands for the picking of blackberries.

Another lesson perhaps, this choice of how to take them.
One by one, tracing their variety on my tongue,
from the bitterness of an unripe red
tightly packed as a nervous heart,
to the rain-bloated looseness of those older,
cobwebbed and dusty as a Claret
laid down for years in a cellar.

Or to hoard them? Piling in the palm
until I cupped a coiled black pearl necklace,
a hedgerow caviar, the bubbles of just poured wine
stilled in my fingers which I'd take together,
each an eye of one great berry, a sudden symphony.

Or as I did just once, strolling towards the low house
growing at the lane's end,
not to eat them at all,
but slowly close my palm into a fist instead,
dissolving their mouthfeel over my skin
and emerging from the hedge and tree tunnel,
my knuckles scratched and my hand blue–black red,
as bloodied as a butcher's or a farmer's at lambing,
or that of a boy who's discovered for the very first time,
just how dark he runs inside.

Joseph Jones

Of course I remember Joseph.
      Fifty press-ups before a night out,
            hair sheened with gel,
                    air dead with scent when he passed.

Told us all how he got his red wings
      over the bandstand railings.
            Her skirt, an umbrella blown inside out,
                white tights shed to high heels.

How he would stand at the bar,
      stroking his chest with one hand,
            drinking with the other;
                the making of a small town myth –

XR2,
    late night fights,
              a trial once
                  with Cardiff Youth.

Late Spring

It made me feel like a man
when I helped my grandfather
castrate the early lambs –

picking the hard orange O-rings
from the plastic bag
and stretching them across the made-to-purpose tool,

heavy and steel-hard in the sun,
while he turned one between his legs
to play it like a cello.

Spreading the pink unwooled skin at their groins
he'd coax them up into the sack,
one-handed, like a man milking,

two soaped beans into a delicate purse,
while gesturing with his other
for the tool, a pliers in reverse,

which I'd pass to him then stand and stare
as he let his clenched fist open
to crown them.

We did the tails too while we were there
so when I walked the field weeks later,
both could be counted;

the tails scattered like catkins among
the windfall of our morning's work –
a strange harvest of the seeds we'd sown.

The Equation

He told me how, after soft afternoons
teaching logarithms and waving away
the blackboard's hieroglyphics with a damp cloth,
he'd return home to the sweet methane of the chicken sheds.

How he'd change from his suit into overalls
and how he dug his hand deep into the bucket
to draw out a leaking fist, which he opened,
a sail of grain unfurling to the birds beneath.

And how later that same hand would flatten
to find a way through the dark
under the sleeping weight of a hen, to bring out,
like a magician whose tricks are just the way of things,

one egg, warm and bald in his brown palm.

Swallows

The swallows are italic again,
cutting their sky-jive
between the telephone wires,
flying in crossed lines.

Their annual regeneration
so flawless to human eyes
that there is no seam
between parent and child.

Just always the swallows
and their script of descenders,
dipping their ink to sign their signatures
across the page of the sky.

On Going

i.m. Jean Sheers

There were instruments, as there always are,
to measure, record and monitor,
windows into the soul's temperature.
But you were disconnected from these

and lay instead an ancient child,
fragile on your side,
your breath working at the skin of your cheek
like a blustery wind at a blind.

There was only one measurement
I needed anyway, which you gave,
triggered by the connection of my kiss
against your paper temple

and registered in the flicker open of your eyes,
in their half-second of recorded understanding
before they disengaged and you slipped back
into the sleep of their slow-closing.

Y Gaer
(The Hill Fort)

Its only defences now, a ring of gorse,
sown yellow in Winter,
its lights diminished come Summer.

Beyond, the mossy gums
of trench and rampart,
gateways that open to the view only

and a stone pile marking the centre,
where my horse threatens beneath me,
jittery from the long gallop,

veins mapping under her skin,
over her twitching muscle;
her nostrils, full of smoking embers.

The land is three-sixty about you here,
an answer to any question, stitched with river silver,
so I think I understand why the man who lost his son

comes here only in bad weather,
when he can lean full tilt
against the wind's shoulder,

take the rain's beating, the hail's pepper-shot
and shout into the storm,
finding at last, something huge enough to blame.

The Hill Fort
(Y Gaer)

On a clear day he'd bring him here,
his young son, charging the hill
as wild as the long-maned ponies

who'd watch a moment
before dropping their heads to graze again.
When he finally got him still

he'd crouch so their eyes were level,
one hand at the small of his back
the other tracing the horizon,

pointing out all the places lived in
by the fathers and sons before them:
Tretower, Raglan, Bredwardine...

And what he meant by this but never said, was
'Look. Look over this land and see how long
the line is before you – how in these generations

we're no more than scattered grains;
that from here in this view, 9, 19 or 90 years
are much the same;

that it isn't the number of steps
that will matter,
but the depth of their impression.'

And that's why he's come back again,
to tip these ashes onto the tongue of the wind
and watch them spindrift into the night.

Not just to make the circle complete,
to heal or mend,
but because he knows these walls,

sunk however low,
still hold him in as well as out:
protect as much as they defend.

Intermission
For L.

A night-long easterly and a chestnut tree
side-swiping the power lines
has stilled the house to this:

wells of darkness in the hallway,
doors opening onto mine shafts of night
and us,

sitting by firelight,
tipping heels of whisky
against the flames and the dust.

An evening of unfamiliar obstacles,
rooms shrunken to the candle's halo,
the world lessened.

You speak from the shore of the other chair,
saying all you really want is to live
long enough to be good at the oboe

and remembering a fly I saw that morning,
vibrating across a window like a tattooist's needle
towards the slip of space that was air not glass,

I think I understand.
That it is after all the small victories that matter,
that are in the end, enough.

Calendar

Spring
Swallows crotchet and
minim the telephone wires,
sing volts down the line.

Summer
Bees go down at the
lips of foxgloves, nervous like
a lover's first time.

Autumn
A spider has danced
a fingerprint in the space
between two branches.

Winter
Nests clot in the veins
of the tree – the rooks are a
passing infection.

Flag

'Each man had a liver, a heart, a brain,
and a *Flag*.
These were his vital organs.
On these his life depended.'

Christopher Logue, *Professor Tucholsky's Facts*

A rail journey westwards is a good place to start,
the country on rewind or fast forward, depending on your seat,
throws up sightings which get more frequent

as the train nears the sea – our flag, strung up on bunting,
hung like wet washing in back yards that echo themselves
down the terraces' hall of mirrors.

Or on the flat end wall of a Swansea gym,
fading to the east where an occasional sun
has ghosted the paint to a bad photocopy.

Or tied to the side of a SNAX caravan,
throwing fits on its pole, high in the motorway wind,
the beast of it struggling to exist.

And so suitable, that dragon,
the currency of legend, the tale
that is truer in its fiction than the facts can ever be:

an old country pulsing to be young
and blessed with a blind spot bigger than itself,
and of course with this flag,

spawning itself west, a strange flower that flourishes best
in the barest of places, or glimpsed above a town hall
on a horizontal pole, wrapped up in itself.

A Chinese burn of red white and green,
a tourniquet, a bandage tight on the wound
staunching the dreams of what might have been.

The Steelworks,

except it doesn't anymore.
A deserted mothership
becalmed on the valley's floor,

sheep passing through the car park,
padlocks rusting on the gates
and birds nesting in the breathless vents.

The work happens elsewhere now,
sometimes all day – men pressing and dipping
in the lifting bays, locking out elbows,

rolling a bicep up an arm then away,
or just kneeling and bowing
to the benediction of a lateral pull.

Pumping iron under strip lights,
they take the strain of another afternoon shift
with screwed tight eyes, pneumatic sighs,

while at the window – still the rain,
rolling off the clouds in sheets
across a brushed-metal sky.

Ebbw Vale, 2002

Song

If we were magpies love,
and some day a bright bait caught your eye
and you were taken in a magpie trap,

a siren in a cage, then I would stay,
perch above you, spread my wings in the rain
and fan you with my feathers in the sun.

And when the others came,
drawn by the oil spill of your plumage,
the darkness of your eye,

I'd watch them strut in,
squawking to their doom
to find themselves trapped.

All night I'd listen to their confusion,
the beat of wing on wire, until the morning
and the farmer came to wring their lives away.

And through the winter I would feed you,
dropping the mites like kisses to your beak.
And in the Spring I'd sing, touch my wings to yours

while we waited for that day
when the farmer, realising at last as all men must
that love is all there is to save,

will open the door to your cage
and let you walk out to me,
where I will be waiting
to help you try your wings again.

Landmark

Afterwards they were timeless
and they lay that way for a while before standing
and dressing, reclaiming their clothes

from the white-blossomed branches of the blackthorn tree.
And already they were part of things again:
his watch, her ear-rings, their clumsy shoes.

They noticed the telephone wires, the time,
even the broken rug of a long-dead sheep
folded at the bottom of the bank.

On going they stopped and turned to look back,
holding each other as if to let go would mean forever,
and they saw where they had been –

a double shadow of green pressed grass, weight imprinted.
A sarcophagus, shallow among the long stems
and complete without them.

Happy Accidents

And Robert Capa, how was he to know?
As the ramps were lowered and the air turned lead
and the marines before him dropped into the water,

that those photographs he took –
no time to set aperture or exposure, just shoot and shoot –
would be printed by some lad, barely sixteen in *Life's* office.

That he'd overheat the negative strips, blister the silver,
melt the emulsion, until their frozen fires caught
and smoked from under the dark room door.

That of the two rolls taken only seven would remain,
their skies heat-blurred, given starbursts of light
and their surfaces grazed to describe so perfectly

the confusion of that day, when a generation's men
stepped out on Europe's shores
to fall headlong through the trapdoor of war.

Drinking with Hitler*
Harare, Zimbabwe, July 2000

He wears his power like an aftershave,
so thick the women about him flounder in it,
their unsure eyes switching in their heads
as they try out their smiles, brief as fireworks on the night.

Turning to me his own slides into place – a CD selected
with play pressed across his lips.
But I've heard about the burned workers' homes,
the scorched huts like cauterised wounds,

the men who cradle the fruit of their bruises,
the 5th brigade trucks that come in the night
and finding no-one in particular,
beat the first two hundred instead.

So finished with me, he turns away
to the Zambian businesswoman at his side –
film pretty, delicate among her jewellery,
long-fingered, dark and quiet.

Conducting asked-for laughter from the bar,
he leans in close, then leaves, as quick as he came
in a flourish of cards,
following his driver out of the door and into his world.

She returns to her drink, lightly touching her leg
where he laid his hand on her thigh,
before looking up into the bar's mirror and washing him away
with one slow blink of her blue-painted eyes.

* The late Dr 'Hitler' Hunzvi, Zanu PF MP and leader
of the Zimbabwe 'War Veterans'

Four Movements in the Scale of Two

I – *Pages*
Cut to us, an overhead shot, early morning.
Lying in bed, foetus curled,
back to naked back.

Opposing bass clefs,
the elegant scars on the hips of a cello,
a butterfly's white wings, resting.

The double heart of a secret fruit,
an 'X' in the equation.
An open book

with blank pages
and nothing on them but sleep,
the reading of our dreams and this.

II – *Still Life*
I sit, eyes closed, my naked back
a canvas on which you paint,

drawing upon a palette of touches,
light across the skin,

shading between my shoulder blades
with the brushstrokes of your hair,

adding depth with the impression of your breasts
against the sentence of my spine

and texture with your tongue
cracking close in my ear,

making me realise once more that bodies, like souls,
only exist when touched.

III – *Eastern Promise*
Beneath the dark tent of her down-falling hair,
Speak he said – and she did.

Drawing the language from deep,
summoning the Steppe and Siberian snow to their bed

until the words caught her
and she cracked their consonants over her tongue

before dropping them to him,
like the shock of new ice in old water.

IV – *Line-Break*
What breaks when this happens?

Insignificant, but enough
to leave a caesura
and us, puzzling over what gave

as suddenly and obscured as a glass
dull-snapping in the hand
beneath the washing water,

that gives no sign it has done so
until the slow smoke-signal of blood,
uncurling from below.

Liable to Floods

'Liable to floods' the farmer warned them.
And on the map, the letters arcing down the valley
in black and white
but still the major wouldn't listen –

tipping back his cap with one finger
and laying a fatherly hand on the farmer's shoulder
'Don't you worry Jack,' he said,
'We've got this one covered.'

And so they made their camp,
a thousand tents across the valley floor,
but even then as the GI's tapped the steel
they felt the backbone of the rock, shallow beneath the soil.

For the next two days they trained
under Moel Siabod's shoulder.
Greenhorns from Kansas, Ohio and Iowa,
sweeping in a line

through the ditches, streams and bracken,
preparing for the landings on Utah and Omaha
pegged as yet to an unknown date
hung somewhere just over the horizon.

On the third night they slept to the sound
of the rain's fusillade and the artillery of thunder,
while outside, under cover of darkness
the river pulled herself up and spread her wings,

bleeding through the camp like ink from a broken cartridge.
The guards were woken by their tin cans and cups
set afloat and clinking against each other
like ghosts in celebration.

They raised the alarm but it was already too late
and the river, arming herself with their rifles,
flushing out the latrines, swallowing the jeeps,
gathered them all and ushered them off.

And as their camp beds became rafts,
gently lifted and spun, more than one GI
woke from dreams of home to sense,
just for a second, somewhere deep in the bone,

how suitable this was,
as if the weather had finally caught up with their lives –
this being taken at night without any say,
this being borne, this being swept away.

History

Lleder Valley, North Wales

Don't try to learn this place
in the pages of a history
but go instead up to the
disused quarry

where the water lies still
and black as oil
and the only chiselling
is that of the blackbird's song

drilling its notes
into the hillside's soil.

And there, beside the falls of moss,
pick yourself a blade of slate,
long as your arm, rusted,
metallic in sound.

Tap it with your heel,
then with your fingertips
at its leaves, gently
prise it apart.

And see how it becomes
a book of slate

in which you can read
a story of stone –
one that's written
throughout this valley,

in every head, across every heart
and down the marrow of every bone.

Amazon

It begins –
Maybe when she's dressing, her fingers tucked
under the wire of her bra.

Or idly in the bath,
their familiar weight
made light of,

or in the mirror, one arm ballerinaed high,
the other testing the water
of her own flesh.

A mote under the skin
settling in her breast,
soft but hard as cartilage, and busy with its own beginning.

*

He tells her kindly enough, and anyway
she knows what is coming, or rather what's already there,

by the way he offers the seat,
his practised look of concern and the slow pace of his voice

that keeps the end of what he has to say
always at arm's length.

She hears the words he uses
and is quietly surprised by how language can do this:

how a certain order can carry so much chaos,
and how that word, with its hard C of cruelty

and soft c of uncertainty,
seems so fitted to the task.

But then she has to leave the surgery
and walk into her new world, so startlingly the same:

the dustbins flowering with rubbish,
shoes for sale at the side of the street and the buses

redding past as if nothing has happened.

*

November 5th and her first outing since,
pale in the Autumn air, the night behind her,
tic-tac sparks from the fire streaming away on the wind.

All of us masked in the flame's hot soul,
writing with sparklers,
our names trailing their furious heads.

Her youngest gives her a bottle of champagne,
one that he's saved for this,
her coming back to us.

It is single-serving size, his size.
She wrings its neck gently, easing it open
but allows him the final give,

the pop and smoky release of its cork,
which he keeps, holding it tight in his fist.
She watches his fingers work around it,

under his coat's pocket, as he feels its shape:
soft but hard, stubborn to the touch, just like the bump
in the middle of the night that started all this in the first place.

*

She's all the way back now,
her life fitting about her once more
like old clothes pulled on from the changing room floor.

But her mind is still faceted, cut from the brink
her body brought it to,
and with it, she dreams.

Sometimes of the weight of its going,
the invisible twin she rises to touch
only to find skin over bone.

Or sometimes of how it was before,
holding sun-curled photos of the past.
But mostly of a day in the future,

when she will choose the nudist night to visit the pool,
where she will walk slow and slim
all the way to the deep end and enter the water an Amazon,

able to draw her bow further and deeper than other women.

Shadow Man

For Mac Adams, Artist

His palette is light,
in all its shades
and the holes it makes.

Conjuring with bulb,
fruit and a shock of grains
spilt across glass,

a dog, resting or dead,
a bird's kinetic moment
in the second before flight

or Karl Marx's head,
born from pebble and stone
into an absence of light.

He works with a darkness
behind his eyes,
understanding as he does

that it's not matter that matters,
or our thoughts and words,
but the shadows they throw

against the lives of others.

Under the Superstition Mountains

'Nothing hiding behind this picket fence...'
                    Eels, *Susan's House*

The Mustang is idle,
out to grass at the side of the road,
absorbing the heat into its mock leather seats.

I sit at the wheel while the photographer sleeps,
reading Lowell on marriage,
the monotonous meanness of his lust

in a suburb-still street in Sun City West
where only the old are allowed to live
and the neighbours keep check on each others' houses.

A man in a track-suit
takes his oxygen tanks for a walk
and a single bird hits a piano wire mid flight,

its note settling without telling
what kind of bird it is,
leaving another space between sense and knowing.

The photographer in the passenger seat
doesn't move, sedated by the heat,
his lower lip dropped

and his finger on the trigger
of the shutter, as if he'd died
and finally shot the perfect still.

Only his breath, deep and dry,
tells me this isn't so, as above us
the Superstition mountains tear an edge off the sky

and somewhere off camera
a rattlesnake uncoils from Winter –
shakes itself alive, without knowing why.

Service

Imagine a theatre, mid-morning, back stage.
Wardrobe are ironing the costumes, a chippy checks a flat
and out front a lone Hoover hums around the table legs
picking up what's left of last night.

This is what it's like.

Boxes left at the door,
the cockles came at two, the oysters at four.

The tables are given skirts
like girls at a prom dress fitting.
Tucked in,
ready to start again.

The Sommelier spits
a boxer's mouthful of red,
lays down the glass
and picks another,
holds it to the light
like a carver,
turning his work in the sun.

Back in the kitchen,
9 am and prep begins.
No longer the off stage corridors of a theatre,
but now a submarine.
Radio on and ten working in here,
at their stations –
Garnish
Hot starters
Meat
Fish
Mousses

Crossing and re-crossing each other
with the knowledge of lovers,
instinctive as matadors, tipping their hips
from the thumb-horns of a carried tray,
a bucket,
a slab of pink salted pork
being taken out back
to be bagged and hung in the water bath
like a regular Houdini.

Outside it's an Autumn morning,
clear air, a yellow leaf falling,
a fag, deeply drawn,
last night's rain drying on the flagstones.
But no time to linger here...

So back through the swing door,
into the kitchen's hot breath,
where a sea bass, lifted from its cool box
where it's been stored all night, upright
just as it would swim,
is laid out, opened with one score of the knife
and its bones unstitched with a pliers
until its flesh reads nothing,
a pink blank page
waiting for nothing
but heat and the tongue.

Behind this a witch's cauldron of onion puree
pops and spits like a New Zealand mud pit,
as 30 duck hams, hung for a week
are parcelled and tied like presents for the tree.

And so it goes:

Salmon piled high like the deckle-edged leaves
of a medieval manuscript.
Oysters shucked and given passion fruit yolks.
Book marks of mackerel, powdered, blown down their seams,
rolled into tigered ballotines.

In pastry the cups are laid out,
2 pence pieces to weigh them down
like coins on the eyes of the dead.
The hot sugar work gets underway;
silicon mat, plastic pin, the tuile mix
rolled flat to see-through sheets.
Heat up,
meat glue brushed,
fish, cubed and cut
all the way to 11.30
and clean down.

A canvas white-washed,
wiped,
ready to start again.

The waiters slip into gold waistcoats,
move about the tables
like sharks through coral reef.

Radio off.

12.45 – the first cover is in.
The ticket machine pokes out its white tongue
which is torn at the root and hung
like a photograph drying in the dark room.

'Check!'

The submarine dives, dives
and the woven walking begins, again.

'Two lamb done – you can go on those!'
Out front a suit unfurls a napkin
over the globe of his stomach,
a sail tacking tight above his belt,
already on the last notch.

The waiter presents a bottle
like a new-born baby.

'Four oysters away!'

Out back the scallops are pinched,
cockles flamed open.

'How long on the chicken?'

The chef stands at the door
performing final checks,
an author, copy-editing the text,
while out front, a father and son take their place.
He's young, fragile, pale,
hair neatly parted as a book open at the centre page.
His father takes a water
his son, a flute of champagne,
one stream of bubbles threading its core,
delicate and finely strung as their conversation.

So, what's the story here?

No one can know for sure,
except that there will be one.

A young chef, got his first job?
A graduate from college?
An army recruit?
A jockey? First race won?

'Done! You can go on that one!'

And the stories go the other way too.
Look at these oysters,
just a few hours ago they were shifting
on the ocean floor,
until a solitary Scottish diver came,

swaying in the night time North Sea
like an idea in a simple giant's mind,
to pick them, and carry them
up through the heavy water
and out into the air,
to here, presented on a plate,
white as snow, smooth as marble
hard as bone.

And so it goes,
until the last cover leaves
and the submarine slows
and the waiters shed their gold,
take a fag outside.

The kitchen is wiped down again,
the casts of food stored.
The washer's sprayer pours,
the tables are stripped
and the Sommelier goes back to his bottles,
picks a long stemmed glass and lifts it to his nose,
a dart player, weighting his arrow,
a gardener, scenting his rose.

The Fishmonger

from the Hungarian original, *Halárus* by István László

This then, is the age of the fishmonger not the fisherman –
his cap tipped as a sergeant's, unsteady on his quiffed head
as he sizes up punters, measuring their movements.

He reaches for a carp as easily as you or I
might dip our hand into a bucket of apples,
feels for the fish, his ingrown nail smarting in the salty water,

and lifts it out, understanding as only he can,
the foil disc of the silver eye, the weight of the blade,
the engine-stroke of his heart, finely tuned to this cruel kindness.

Understanding as only he can, the spot between the knuckles
where a nail might enter as if through butter,
how to slice flesh as others cut celery,

how to pare his speech as he might men
were he hurt and pushed to fight.
But like a tree hit by lightning, there is no healing bark

about his struck heart and the wood at the trunk's centre
pulses and gasps for growth like a fish
struggling for its last breath as if biting the air for water.

Stitch in Time

And so he left his wife, just 15 years old, in Gujarat
and travelled back

across three seas
to Fiji and the Garden Island of Taveuni,

where he bent once more
to the cloth, spilling from the bench onto the floor

and moved about the dummy's baste
like a musician round his double bass.

Where, by the hurricane lamp's sepia,
he was the cutter, coatmaker and finisher,

checking again and again his stab and pad stitch,
the depth of the gorge, the sleeve's angle of pitch –

a bespoke suit for the local chief,
who was offering (he thinks of his wife, his wife)

an acre of ground – his own piece of land
for this man of cloth, made by his hand.

And when they told him where it lay – about the 180 degrees,
the invisible meridian that came over the hill through the
coconut trees,

the imaginary chalk mark where here, tomorrow starts,
and here, today is ending, he felt it in his heart.

The pin-stripe of longitude, the balance, the symmetry,
bisecting time and space, he understood it immediately.

And so ten years later when he returned for his wife
he brought her back to show her the life

he'd built around that line: the corrugated Meridian Store,
the Meridian Cinema, its screen lifting from the floor

to reveal a boxing ring every Saturday night.
Then later, the Meridian Garage, with his taxis' headlights

shaking into the dark, sweeping across the bay.
Even the sign was his, with its arrows pointing each way

where tourists stood to have their photo taken, a foot each side,
where the future started and the present died.

And that's why, four daughters and a son later, when
his joints were as stiff as his oldest scissors, he went to London

and on his first morning there,
walked alone through the morning air

to Greenwich, to see at last where it all started.
To stand under a blue sky where the swallows darted:

an explorer discovering the source, the still point after the strife,
the first stitch in the pattern to which he'd cut his life.

L.A. Evening

'E. Booth heard the solemn whisper of the god of all arts.
"I shall give you hunger and pain and sleepless nights, also
beauty and satisfaction known to few, and glimpses of the
heavenly life. None of these shall you have continually, and of
their coming and going you shall not be foretold"'
                    The Players Club, *Edward Booth's Legacy*

It's at this time of day,
when the rollerbladers pass her window
and the sirens start somewhere far below
and the sun leaks into the ocean,
that she sits to the screening of her photographs.

Scenes from every stage of her life:
Olivier, holding her Ophelia,
then again with her slave girl
and Brando, swinging her Salvation Army Sarah
as if he'd just caught her.
Two with the queen – mother and daughter.

She looks at them as the sun turns off
and the lights come up in the city of angels.
Freeze frames, silent films in which
the actors wear the faces of her friends
and speak in the off-screen voices
of those who have left her now, alone with the audience.

As always she leaves
before the roll call of the credits.
Tunes the dimmer switch into the night,
lets the dog in, puts the cats out –
checks the sensitivity of the intruder light.

The Singing Men

They are the singing men. Every city has them,
singing for their supper or just for the hell of it.

Corners and doorways are good places to find them,
on the edges of things, humming, humming.

Or full-throated, singing to swallow the moon,
the tendons in their necks making valleys in their stubble

and the songs from memory,
from a time when they weren't just the singing men

but had lives, in which, if they were lucky, they'd squeeze
a little music in, between the lovers, the kids, the wives.

But now it's just the songs that are left
to keep them threaded to the earth,

the world's greatest group, toting love ballads on the
                                        Staten Island ferry,
slave songs in New Jersey, folk in Moscow, blues in Leeds

and of course here, on the edge of the underground,
singing opera on the steps of Balham tube,

his solos resounding down to the ticket barriers' greyhound stalls
and his costume perfect – one gold can of Extra,

beard scribbled over his chin, dirt like grain in the wood,
as he sits there, legs open, welcoming the commuters home.

The Wake

He looks me straight in the eye,
ninety years old,
folded into his favourite chair

and tells me he doesn't want this,
to watch himself die, to have the doctor
plumb any further in the depths of his scarred lungs.

He, who himself spent so many years
holding the chests of others up to the light
to forecast the storms gathering there,

the squalls and depressions
smudging those two pale oceans,
rising and falling in the rib cage's hull.

Here then is the old curse
of too much knowledge, driftwood
collected along the shore of a century.

He settles himself in the chair
and I say what I can, but my words are spoken
into a coastal wind long after the ship has sailed.

Later he shows me to the door
and as he stands in its frame to wave me away
we both know there has already been a passing,

one that has left a wake as that of a great ship
that disturbs the sea for miles either side
but leaves the water directly at its stern

strangely settled, turned, fresh
and somehow new,
like the first sea there ever was

or that ever will be.

Skirrid Fawr

Just like the farmers who once came to scoop
handfuls of soil from her holy scar,

so I am still drawn to her back for the answers
to every question I have never known.

To the sentence of her slopes,
the blunt wind glancing from her withers,

to the split view she reveals
with every step along her broken spine.

This edge of her cleft palate,
part hill, part field,

rising from a low mist, a lonely hulk
adrift through Wales.

Her east-west flanks, one dark, one sunlit,
her vernacular of borders.

Her weight, the unspoken words
of an unlearned tongue.